VALUABLE U.S. ERROR COIN GUIDE 2025

The Complete Visual Handbook Featuring Over 120 High-Resolution Images to Help You Identify Mint Mistakes Worth Money

LUCAS FORD

All rights reserved. No part of this publication may be reproduced, distributed, or transmitted in any form or by any means, including photocopying, recording, or other electronic or mechanical methods, without the prior written permission of the publisher, except in the case of brief quotations embodied in critical reviews and certain other noncommercial uses permitted by copyright law.

Copyright © Lucas Ford, 2025.

TABLE OF CONTENTS

INTRODUCTION 5

CHAPTER 1 7

  THE FUNDAMENTALS OF ERROR COINS 7

    What Makes a Coin an "Error"? 7

    Types of Mint Errors 9

    Age Does Not Always Equal Value: Understanding Market Dynamics 10

    Rarity vs. Demand: What Drives Value 11

CHAPTER 2 13

  ESSENTIAL EQUIPMENT AND SKILLS 13

    Tools of the Trade 13

CHAPTER 3 15

  MASTERING COIN GRADING 15

    Understanding the Sheldon Scale 15

    Major Grading Services 18

CHAPTER 4 21

  CONSERVATION AND PRESERVATION 21

    Essential Storage Solutions 21

    Professional Preservation Methods 22

    Critical Preservation Guidelines 22

    Best Practices for Handling 23

CHAPTER 5 24

  ERROR COINS BY DENOMINATION 24

    Valuable Lincoln Cent Errors 24

    Valuable Jefferson Nickel Errors 39

    Valuable Roosevelt Dime Errors 49

    Valuable Washington Quarter Errors 52

    Valuable Kennedy Half-Dollar Errors 59

CHAPTER 6 63
MARKET NAVIGATION 63
Price Guides and Resources 63
Where To Sell Your Coins 64
CHAPTER 7 66
Strategies for Selling Your Error Coins 66
BONUS CHAPTER 68
APPENDICES 70
Glossary of Terms and Definitions 70

INTRODUCTION

In 2014, a beginning collector purchased a handful of Lincoln pennies for $5 at a local flea market. Among them was a 1971 Doubled Die Lincoln Cent – a coin that would later sell for $14,950. Stories like this aren't just lucky accidents; they're the result of knowing exactly what to look for.

Have you ever wondered if that odd-looking coin in your change could be worth thousands? Or maybe you've passed up valuable errors simply because you weren't sure what made them special? I've spent over three decades hunting these treasures, and I'm here to tell you: the next great find could be sitting in your pocket right now.

Welcome to the "**Valuable U.S. Error Coin Guide 2025**," your definitive companion in the fascinating world of numismatic errors. Whether you're examining coins from your pocket change or considering a significant investment in a major error variety, this guide was crafted with one purpose: to transform uncertainty into confidence.

Too often, I've encountered collectors who passed by valuable errors simply because they didn't know what to look for, or worse, parted with rare pieces for a fraction of their worth due to lack of knowledge. This guide changes that narrative. Drawing from my experiences as a seasoned numismatist and error coin specialist, I've distilled decades of expertise into clear, actionable insights that will serve both novice collectors and seasoned veterans alike.

Within these pages, you'll find more than just listings and valuations. You'll discover the stories behind the errors, the technical details that matter, and most importantly, the confidence to identify, evaluate, and appreciate these numismatic treasures. I've structured this guide to be both comprehensive and accessible, eliminating the guesswork that often accompanies error coin collecting.

From the modest beginnings of examining pocket change to authenticating major mint errors at national conventions, my journey has taught me that every collector's path is unique. This guide honors that diversity by providing multiple entry points to the hobby, whether you're starting with Lincoln cents or diving straight into dollar varieties.

The market for error coins continues to evolve, driven by new discoveries, changing collector preferences, and advancing authentication techniques. This 2025 edition incorporates the latest market trends, recently discovered varieties, and updated valuations to ensure you have the most current information at your fingertips.

Remember, every significant collection started with a single discovery. Let this guide be your companion in making those discoveries, whether you're searching through rolls of cents or bidding at major auctions. The thrill of finding an unmarked rarity or identifying an overlooked error never diminishes – it's what keeps us passionate about this fascinating corner of numismatics.

Welcome to your journey in error coin collecting. The treasures are out there, waiting to be discovered. Let's find them together.

CHAPTER 1

THE FUNDAMENTALS OF ERROR COINS

What Makes a Coin an "Error"?

Imagine a perfect symphony where every musician plays their part flawlessly. Now picture what happens when one instrument hits an unexpected note – that's similar to how coin errors occur in the otherwise precise world of minting. A mint error is any deviation from a coin's intended design, specification, or composition that occurred during the official minting process.

However, not every unusual-looking coin is an error. Let's break down what qualifies as a genuine mint error:

Official Mint Production Requirements

- The coin must have been produced at an official U.S. Mint facility
- The error must have occurred during the minting process
- The coin must have been released into circulation or escaped quality control measures

Key Characteristics of Genuine Mint Errors

- Repeatable patterns (in the case of die errors)
- Consistent metal composition
- Evidence of authentic mint production methods
- No signs of post-mint manipulation

What's NOT Considered a Mint Error

Post-mint damage (PMD)

- Scratches from circulation
- Environmental damage
- Intentional alterations
- Chemical treatment
- Heat damage

Machine-made alterations

- Pressed or rolled coins
- Drilled or punched holes
- Counterstamped pieces

Common Signs of Authentic Errors

- Metal flow lines consistent with mint production
- Original mint luster in protected areas
- Natural metal displacement patterns
- Consistent weight (within acceptable range for error type)
- Die characteristics matching known mint practices

Authentication Tips for Beginners

- Compare suspected errors with verified examples
- Check for signs of artificial alteration
- Examine metal flow and strike characteristics
- Consider having valuable pieces authenticated by reputable services:

  - Professional Coin Grading Service (PCGS)

  - Numismatic Guaranty Corporation (NGC)

  - ANACS

  - Independent Coin Graders (ICG)

Remember: True mint errors are products of specific manufacturing processes gone wrong. Understanding these processes is crucial for distinguishing genuine errors from damaged or altered coins. In the following sections, we'll explore the fascinating world of die, planchet, and strike errors in detail.

Types of Mint Errors

1. Die Errors

Die errors occur during the production or use of the dies that stamp designs onto coins. These are among the most collectible errors because they often create multiple identical pieces.

Common Die Errors:

- Doubled Dies
- Die Cracks
- Die Chips
- Repunched Mint Marks

2. Planchet Errors

Planchet errors happen before the coin is struck, involving problems with the blank metal disc (planchet) that becomes the coin.

Types of Planchet Errors:

- Wrong Planchet
- Clipped Planchet
- Lamination Errors
- Wrong Metal

3. Strike Errors

Strike errors occur during the actual striking process when the die meets the planchet.

Major Strike Error Types:

- Off-Center Strikes

- Multiple Strikes
- Broadstrikes
- Indent Strikes

Value Factors for All Error Types:

Denomination (higher denominations typically more valuable)

- Error percentage/severity
- Grade/condition
- Rarity of error type
- Historical significance
- Visual appeal

Remember: The key to identifying valuable errors is understanding how they were made. This knowledge helps distinguish genuine mint errors from post-mint damage or alteration.

Age Does Not Always Equal Value: Understanding Market Dynamics

One of the most common misconceptions in error coin collecting is that older automatically means more valuable. Let me share a surprising truth: a 2004 Wisconsin State Quarter with an extra leaf, barely two decades old, can command $6,000, while many Lincoln cent errors from the 1940s might fetch only $20-$30.

The real drivers of an error coin's value lie in its story, rarity, and collector demand. Take the 1955 Doubled Die Lincoln Cent – its significant value isn't primarily due to its age, but rather its perfect storm of characteristics: it was widely publicized, easily identifiable, and occurred on a popular coin series. In contrast, some doubled dies from the 1920s sell for far less, despite being older and technically rarer.

Modern errors can be extraordinarily valuable, particularly those from popular series or with dramatic visual appeal. The State Quarter program (1999-2008) produced several highly sought-after errors, with some pieces selling for thousands of dollars. Why? Because these errors occurred during a time of peak collecting interest, on a series that captured the public's imagination.

The advent of third-party grading services and population reports has also transformed how we value error coins. Today's market places greater emphasis on error type, visual impact, and preservation quality than on age alone. A spectacular off-center strike from 2020 might outvalue a subtle die crack from 1890 simply because it offers more visual drama and collecting appeal.

Consider this: improved quality control at modern mints actually makes some new errors rarer than their vintage counterparts. When an error does escape today's sophisticated detection systems, it often represents a more significant deviation from the norm, potentially making it more desirable to collectors.

What truly matters in today's market:

- The visual impact of the error
- The popularity of the base coin series
- The number of similar errors known to exist
- The quality of preservation
- The historical significance or story behind the error
- Current collector trends and interests

Understanding these market dynamics helps collectors make smarter decisions. Whether you're examining a Civil War-era coin or last year's issue, focus on the error's distinctive characteristics rather than its age. In error collecting, every decade has its treasures – you just need to know where to look.

Rarity vs. Demand: What Drives Value

In the fascinating world of error coins, an intriguing paradox often emerges: some of the rarest errors struggle to find buyers, while more common varieties command premium prices. To understand this phenomenon, let's explore the delicate dance between rarity and demand.

Consider the 1969-S Doubled Die Lincoln Cent. With fewer than 100 known examples, it's extraordinarily rare, and pieces regularly sell for over $100,000. Yet other doubled dies of similar rarity might struggle to break $1,000. The difference? The 1969-S benefits from intense collector demand, driven by its status as a legendary rarity in the popular Lincoln cent series.

Demand is shaped by multiple factors that go beyond mere scarcity. Eye appeal plays a crucial role – errors that are easily visible and dramatic often attract more interest than subtle varieties that require magnification to appreciate. This explains why a boldly struck 40% off-center quarter might sell for more than a technically rarer but less obvious die crack variety.

Marketing and publicity also significantly influence demand. When a major error makes headlines or gets featured in numismatic publications, it often creates a surge of collector interest. The 2004 Wisconsin "Extra Leaf" Quarter errors became numismatic superstars not just because of their rarity, but because of the media attention they received and their easily recognizable nature.

The collector base for the original series also impacts demand. Error coins from popular series like Lincoln Cents, Morgan Dollars, or State Quarters typically command higher prices than similar errors from less collected series. A spectacular error on a Susan B. Anthony Dollar, despite its rarity, might generate less excitement simply because fewer collectors focus on this series.

Authentication and documentation play increasingly important roles in today's market. Well-documented errors with clear provenance and third-party certification often command significant premiums over similar pieces lacking such pedigrees. This is particularly true for major rarities where authenticity concerns could significantly impact value.

The sweet spot in error coin values often occurs when rarity and demand align perfectly. This happens when an error is scarce enough to be special but not so rare that collectors lose hope of acquiring one. The 1955 Doubled Die Cent exemplifies this balance – rare enough to be valuable, yet with sufficient examples available that collectors can realistically hope to own one.

Remember: while rarity provides the foundation for value, it's collector demand that ultimately determines price. Smart collectors understand this relationship and look for errors that combine genuine scarcity with strong collector appeal. In the end, the most valuable error coins are often those that tell the most compelling stories to the largest number of interested collectors.

CHAPTER 2

ESSENTIAL EQUIPMENT AND SKILLS

Tools of the Trade

While your eyes can spot dramatic error coins like off-centers or wrong metals, the true treasures of error collecting often hide in plain sight. Many valuable varieties lurk unseen in everyday pocket change, waiting for the collector with the right tools and knowledge to discover them. Success in error coin hunting isn't just about having expensive equipment – it's about having the right tools and knowing how to use them effectively.

Essential Starter Kit:

1. Reference Materials

- A comprehensive error coin guide (like this book)
- Access to trusted online resources
- High-quality photographs of known varieties
- Price guides for current market values

2. Magnification Equipment

- Start with a quality 5x lens for grading ($8-10)
- Add a 10x Hastings Triplet for variety hunting ($20-40)
- Consider 14x for detailed examination
- Optional: 20x for specialized variety verification

Pro Tip: Avoid the "metal monsters" (standard 16x magnifiers) – they offer poor optics and actually only provide about 10x magnification despite their claims.

3. Lighting Setup

- Adjustable desk lamp with soft-white bulb
- Goose-neck style lamp (ideal for maneuverability)
- Position light source close to examination area
- Ensure ability to angle light for optimal viewing
- Even a basic 75-watt living room lamp can work if properly positioned

4. Digital Scale

- Small, accurate pocket scale (available at most retail stores)
- Precision to at least 0.1 grams
- Used for weight verification of error types
- Budget-friendly options available ($15-20)

5. Proper Technique

- Position magnifier at correct distance from eye
- Maintain appropriate spacing between lens and coin
- Use proper lighting angle for maximum surface reflection
- Practice proper handling to avoid damage
- Learn to systematically examine coin surfaces

Remember: While high-end equipment can be helpful, many successful error coin hunters started with basic tools. Focus on mastering proper technique with entry-level equipment before investing in more expensive options. The key is developing your eye and understanding what to look for – tools simply help confirm what your knowledge suggests might be there.

Advanced collectors may want to expand their toolkit over time, but don't feel pressured to buy everything at once. Start with the basics: a good 10x magnifier, proper lighting, and reliable reference materials. As your expertise grows, you'll naturally discover which additional tools will benefit your specific collecting interests.

CHAPTER 3

MASTERING COIN GRADING

Understanding the Sheldon Scale

In the world of numismatics, a coin's condition often speaks louder than its age or rarity. Developed by Dr. William Sheldon in the 1940s, the Sheldon Grading Scale has become the cornerstone of modern coin grading. This numerical system, ranging from 1 to 70, transforms the subjective art of condition assessment into a standardized science that guides both collectors and dealers in determining a coin's true value.

The Foundation of Modern Grading

The genius of the Sheldon Scale lies in its precision. While earlier systems used broad descriptive terms, Sheldon's numerical approach allows for subtle distinctions in condition that can mean thousands of dollars in value difference. The scale wasn't just revolutionary – it became the universal language of coin collecting.

Mastering the Scale

1. Poor to Fair (P-1 to FR-2)

- Barely identifiable coins
- Date may be worn smooth
- Major design elements heavily worn
- Often collected for historical significance

2. Good to Very Good (G-4 to VG-10)

- Major design elements visible but worn
- Lettering partially visible but legible
- Rims must be mostly intact
- Common starting point for budget collectors

3. Fine to Very Fine (F-12 to VF-35)

- Clear design details emerge
- Moderate wear becomes uniform
- All major features distinct
- Popular grade for type collecting

4. Extremely Fine to About Uncirculated (EF-40 to AU-58)

- Light wear on highest points
- Most mint luster gone
- Sharp design details
- Transitional grades to uncirculated status

Uncirculated Grades (MS-60 to MS-70)

The Mint State (MS) grades represent coins that never entered circulation, though they may show varying degrees of handling marks:

5. Commercial Uncirculated (MS-60 to MS-63)

- No wear, but numerous contact marks
- May show weak strikes or spotting
- Original mint luster present
- Entry-level investment grade

6. Choice Uncirculated (MS-64 to MS-66)

- Fewer contact marks
- Strong eye appeal
- Above-average strike
- Premium investment quality

7. Superb Uncirculated (MS-67 to MS-70)

- Exceptional eye appeal
- Minimal imperfections
- Nearly perfect to perfect strikes
- Top-tier investment pieces

Special Considerations for Error Coins

When grading error coins, the Sheldon Scale takes on additional complexity. The grade must consider:

- The error's prominence
- Strike quality of both normal and error elements
- Overall surface preservation
- Uniqueness of the error type

Modern Applications

Today's professional grading services have refined the Sheldon Scale further by:

- Adding "plus" grades (e.g., MS-64+)
- Including color designations for copper coins
- Noting special attributes like Full Bands or Full Steps
- Implementing "star" designations for exceptional eye appeal

Impact on Value

Understanding the Sheldon Scale is crucial because a single grade point difference can significantly affect value. For example, a rare date Morgan Dollar might be worth $5,000 in MS-63 but command $25,000 in MS-65. This exponential value increase demonstrates why mastering the grading scale is essential for serious collectors.

Remember: While the Sheldon Scale provides a framework, grading remains both an art and a science. Experience, careful study, and guidance from professional graders are invaluable in developing your grading skills.

Major Grading Services

The cornerstone of any coin collection's value lies in its grading. While factors like rarity and historical significance play important roles, a coin's grade often becomes the decisive factor in determining its worth. In the United States, four prestigious third-party grading (TPG) services stand as the gatekeepers of coin authentication and grading standards.

Leading the field are the **Professional Coin Grading Service (PCGS)** and the **Numismatic Guaranty Corporation (NGC)**, followed by **Independent Coin Graders (ICG)** and **ANACS**. Each of these organizations maintains comprehensive certification databases that dealers and collectors can reference to verify a coin's authenticity and grade. Though these names appear frequently in coin listings and at auctions, their inner workings and distinctions remain a mystery to many collectors. Let's pull back the curtain and explore what makes each of these grading services unique.

The Professional Coin Grading Service

P.O. Box 9458

Newport Beach, CA 92658

Phone: 800-447-8848

e-mail: info@pcgs.com

www.PCGS.com

The Professional Coin Grading Service (PCGS) stands as a titan in the numismatic world. Since its establishment in 1986 by David Hall and six other visionary collectors, PCGS has grown from a domestic grading service into a global authority, with operations spanning across Europe and Asia.

Their comprehensive services extend beyond basic grading. The company offers multiple tiers of authentication, from their standard grading service to their premium Secure Plus option. They've also embraced modern technology with their Tru-View system, providing high-resolution photography that captures every nuance of a coin's condition.

Perhaps PCGS's greatest achievement is the level of trust they've earned within the collecting community. The sight of a PCGS holder, often called a "slab" by collectors, has become synonymous with quality and authenticity. In fact, the mere presence of a PCGS slab can significantly enhance a coin's market value, reflecting the weight that collectors and dealers place on their certification.

The Numismatic Guaranty Corporation

P.O. Box 4776

Sarasota, FL 34230

United States

Phone: 1-800-NGC-COIN

Service@NGCcoin.com

www.NGCcoin.com

When it comes to coin grading giants, the Numismatic Guaranty Corporation (NGC) stands shoulder-to-shoulder with PCGS at the pinnacle of the industry. With over 30 million coins graded, NGC has earned the distinction of being the world's largest coin grading service by volume. Their credibility is further cemented by their longstanding role as the official grading service of the American Numismatic Association (ANA), a position they've held since 1995.

NGC maintains stringent standards, taking a firm stance against grading modified coins – a policy that has helped build their sterling reputation. Their connection to the ANA, combined with their rigorous authentication processes, means that an NGC certification often translates directly into enhanced market value for certified coins.

Independent Coin Graders

8120 Anderson Road, Suite 101

Tampa, FL 33634

Phone: 877-221-4424

E-mail: customersatisfaction@icgcoin.com

www.icgcoin.com

Independent Coin Graders (ICG), though a relative newcomer to the grading scene since 1998, has carved out a unique niche in the numismatic world. Unlike PCGS and NGC, ICG maintains a laser focus on grading services, deliberately staying out of the coin trading business to maintain absolute objectivity.

What sets ICG apart is their combination of competitive pricing and notably conservative grading standards. By offering lower fees than their larger competitors, they've become the go-to choice for budget-conscious collectors seeking professional certification.

Perhaps ICG's most distinctive characteristic is their famously conservative grading approach. This cautious methodology has earned them a special reputation among serious collectors, who appreciate that an ICG-graded coin typically performs above its assigned grade rather than below it. This built-in "safety margin" has become one of their strongest selling points.

ANACS

P.O. Box 6000

Englewood, CO 80155

Phone: 800.888.1861

CustomerService@ANACS.com

www.ANACS.com

Standing as a pioneer in coin certification, ANACS (American Numismatic Association Certification Service) has been the bedrock of professional coin grading since 1972. Their decades of experience in authenticating coins, medals, and tokens have established them as a trusted name in the industry. With a reputation built on exceptional staff expertise and customer service, combined with competitive pricing, ANACS makes professional grading accessible to collectors of all levels. Their streamlined submission process, requiring only a simple form and secure shipping, exemplifies their commitment to user-friendly service.

The importance of third-party grading cannot be overstated in today's collecting landscape. Whether you choose ANACS (anacs.com) or any other major grading service, professional certification serves a dual purpose: it authenticates your coins while potentially enhancing their market value. This independent verification provides both collectors and buyers with the confidence that comes from knowing exactly what they own or are purchasing. In today's numismatic market, this peace of mind has become not just valuable, but essential.

CHAPTER 4

CONSERVATION AND PRESERVATION

The difference between a valuable error coin and a damaged curiosity often comes down to one crucial factor: preservation. As stewards of numismatic history, our responsibility extends beyond merely finding these treasures – we must ensure they survive for future generations of collectors.

Essential Storage Solutions

Individual Coin Protection

The foundation of proper coin storage begins with individual protection. The industry standard "2x2" holders (named for their two-inch square dimensions) provide excellent protection for single specimens. These holders, often called "flips" by collectors, offer several advantages:

- Clear visibility for examination
- Space for labeling and documentation
- Protection against environmental factors
- Easy storage and organization

Bulk Storage Options

For larger collections, especially those containing multiple coins of the same denomination, coin tubes offer an efficient storage solution. These inexpensive plastic containers:

- Hold complete rolls of specific denominations
- Prevent coins from mixing with general circulation
- Provide sturdy protection during transport
- Include space for labeling and organization

Professional Preservation Methods

Slabbing Services

Professional grading services offer perhaps the ultimate in coin preservation through a process known as "slabbing." This service provides:

- Tamper-resistant plastic encapsulation
- Professional grading and attribution
- Long-term preservation
- -Enhanced marketability for future sales
- Independent verification of authenticity

Modern Documentation Tools

Technology has introduced new ways to document and study coins while maintaining their preservation:

- PhoneScope and similar devices allowing 60x magnification
- Digital photography capabilities
- Ability to share images with experts remotely
- Permanent record of condition and characteristics

Critical Preservation Guidelines

The Golden Rule: Never Clean Your Coins

This cannot be emphasized enough: Never attempt to clean a coin. Here's why:

- Any form of cleaning can damage the coin's surface
- Natural patina is preferred by collectors
- Cleaning reduces numismatic value
- Cleaned coins are difficult to sell
- Even professional cleaning diminishes value

Environmental Considerations

Proper storage environment is crucial:

- Maintain consistent temperature

- Control humidity levels
- Avoid direct sunlight
- Keep away from chemicals and pollutants
- Store in a secure, stable location

Best Practices for Handling

General Handling Rules
- Hold coins by their edges
- Work over a soft surface
- Use clean, dry hands
- Avoid touching the face of the coin
- Handle in adequate lighting

When Additional Protection is Needed
Consider professional encapsulation when:

- The coin has significant value
- Long-term storage is planned
- Authentication is desired
- Sale of the coin is anticipated
- The error type is particularly fragile

Remember: The goal of preservation isn't just to maintain value – it's to ensure these fascinating pieces of minting history survive for future generations of collectors to study and enjoy. Every error coin tells a unique story of its creation, and proper preservation ensures that story can continue to be told.

CHAPTER 5

ERROR COINS BY DENOMINATION

Valuable Lincoln Cent Errors

The Lincoln Cent – America's longest-running coin design and perhaps its most carefully scrutinized. Since 1909, billions of these humble pennies have rolled off the mint's presses, but among these countless coins lie some of numismatics' most fascinating and valuable treasures. While most Lincoln cents in your pocket might be worth exactly one cent, certain mint errors in this series have commanded prices that would make even seasoned collectors do a double-take – from the legendary 1955 Doubled Die that regularly sells for tens of thousands of dollars to the elusive 1922 No D that continues to captivate error hunters.

Whether you're searching through bank rolls or inherited collections, knowing what to look for in Lincoln cent errors could quite literally mean the difference between pocket change and life-changing discoveries. Some of the most valuable finds in recent years have come from everyday people who simply knew what they were looking at. So, let's explore these fascinating mistakes that have become numismatic gold.

1959 D Mule Penny

Known as the 1959-D Wheat Reverse "Mule," this controversial error features something that shouldn't exist – a 1959 Denver Mint penny with the old wheat stalks reverse design instead of the Lincoln Memorial. While its authenticity has been debated (including a claim of forgery by Mark Hofmann), what matters for collectors is knowing what to look for: a 1959-D Lincoln cent that shows wheat stalks on the reverse instead of the Memorial design. Despite questions about its authenticity, this unique piece sold for **$31,050** at auction, demonstrating the premium collectors will pay for potentially significant minting errors.

1960 D Over D, Small Over Large Date Penny, Repunched Mint Mark

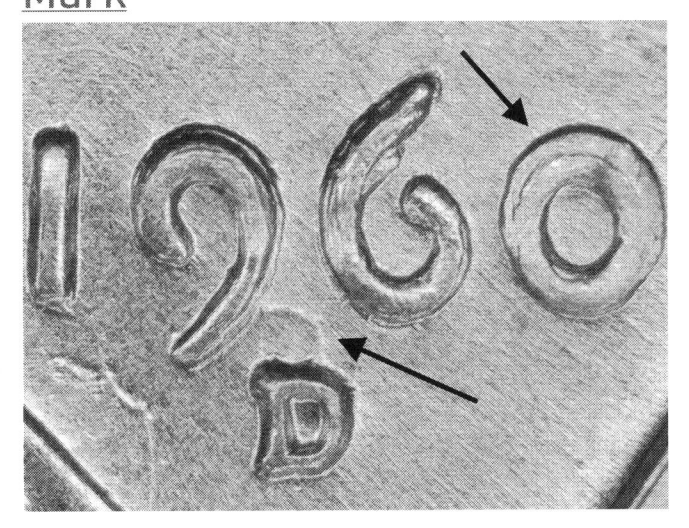

The 1960-D Lincoln Cent has two key errors worth searching for. Check the mint mark with a magnifying glass for a faint "D" beneath the main "D." Also examine the date carefully - you're looking for clear doubling in the numbers from a Small Date being struck over a Large Date. Values range from **$2** for basic brown specimens up to **$1,375** for pristine red examples in MS66+ grade.

1961 Penny, Re-punched Mint Mark

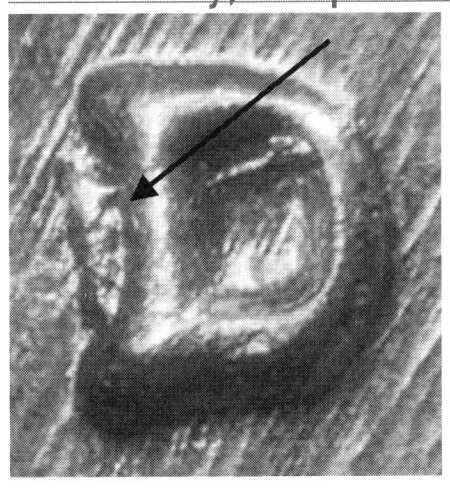

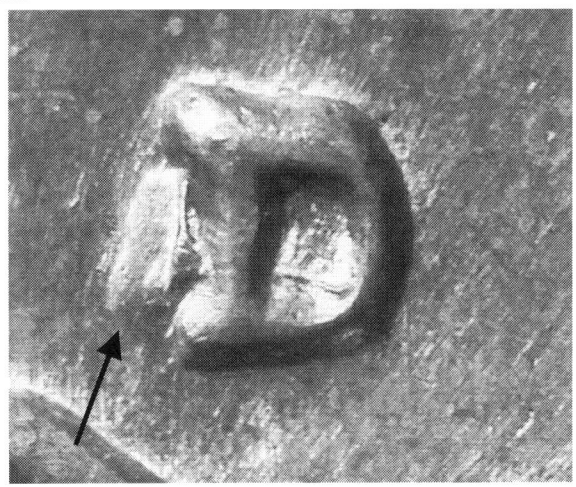

The 1961-D Lincoln Cent features hand-punched mint mark errors. Under magnification, look for a second "D" that appears either sideways, upside-down, or in the wrong position beneath the correctly positioned D. Most examples sell for **$3-$5**, but the D/Horizontal D variety brings **$10-$60**, with pristine red specimens reaching **$228**.

1962 D Penny, Full Brockage Reverse

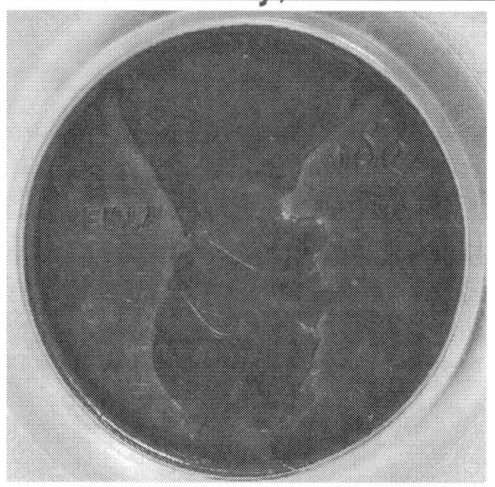

The 1962-D Lincoln Cent has a rare "full brockage reverse" error. Instead of the Lincoln Memorial on the back, look for a mirror image of Lincoln's portrait (reversed and indented). Despite showing wear, one example graded AU53 sold for over **$500.**

1963 D Penny, Double Die Obverse

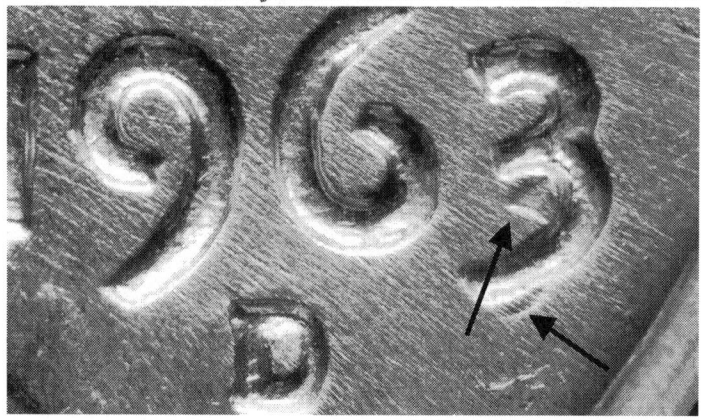

The 1963-D Lincoln Cent has a Double Die Obverse error. Using magnification, look for clear doubling on the number "3" in the date. Values range from **$25-30** in MS62 condition, with the finest MS65 example selling for **$209**.

1964 No Mint Mark Penny Struck on Clad Dime Planchet

The 1964 Philadelphia Lincoln Cent has a "wrong planchet" error. Look for a penny struck on a smaller dime planchet, causing the design to be cut off at the edges. One MS64 example sold for **$5,750**.

1965 Penny Mirrored Obverse Die Cap Error

The 1965 Lincoln Cent has a "mirrored obverse die cap" error. Look for a coin with a normal front but a back that shows a blurry, reversed image of the front design bleeding through. In MS65 Red condition, this error sold for **$1,800**.

1966 Penny, Retained Strike-Through

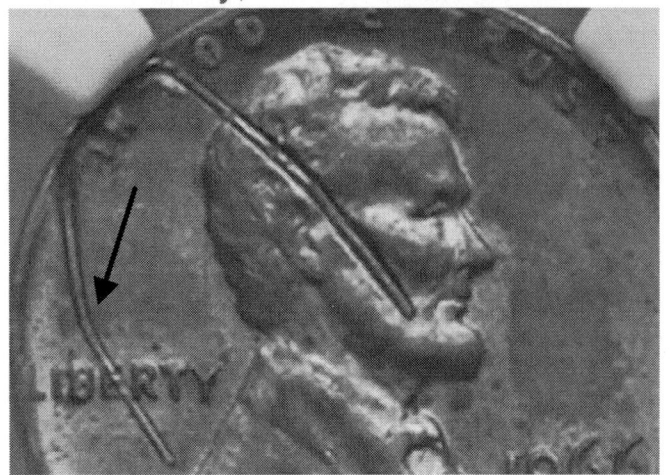

The 1966 Lincoln Cent has a "retained strike-through" error. Look for a coin showing clear impressions of foreign objects (like staples, string, wire, or wood) embedded in its surface during striking. These rare errors can sell for around **$1,150**.

1968 Penny, DDR and DDO

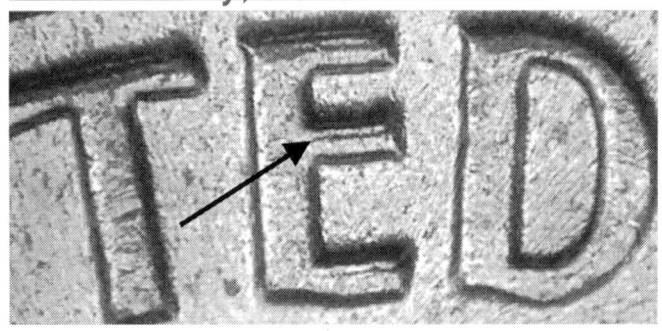

The 1968-D Lincoln Cent has Double Die Reverse (DDR) and Double Die Obverse (DDO) errors. Using magnification, look for clear doubling in the design - the more obvious the doubling, the more valuable the coin. A red MS65 DDR example sold for **$285** in 2023.

1969 S Double Die Obverse Penny Error

The 1969-S Lincoln Cent has a dramatic Double Die Obverse error. Under magnification, look for strong doubling in "LIBERTY," "IN GOD WE TRUST," and the date. With only 40-50 known examples, this rare error is highly valuable - an MS64 Red specimen was valued at **$126,500**. Be cautious of counterfeits as this error is frequently forged.

1970-D Penny Struck 55% Off-Centre

The 1971 Lincoln Cent has an "off-center" error. Look for coins where part of the design is missing because the planchet was misaligned during striking - this example was struck 55% off-center. In MS63 Red condition, this error sold for **$65**.

1972 Penny, Doubled Die Obverse

The 1972 Lincoln Cent has a Double Die Obverse error. Using magnification, look for clear doubling in "LIBERTY," "IN GOD WE TRUST," and the date. Values range from **$295** to **$14,400** depending on condition and color.

1974 "S" Penny with a Die Break Error

The 1974-S Lincoln Cent has a die break error. Look for a visible piece missing from the design on either side of the coin - this is different from circulation damage. A pristine example can be worth up to **$184.**

1975 Penny Fold-Over Error

The 1975 Lincoln Cent has a "fold-over" error. Look for coins shaped like a half circle where the planchet was folded during striking, with partial design elements visible. Values range from **$575** for authenticated pieces to **$1,495** in MS65 Red-Brown condition.

1976 Penny, Off-center

The 1976 Lincoln Cent has "off-center" strike errors. Look for coins with partial blank surfaces where the design shifted during striking. Values vary by how off-center the strike is: 5-10% brings up to **$10**, 50% with visible date brings **$50-$110**, and 80% off-center with visible date can reach **$185-$230**.

1978 Penny Struck on a Dime - Double Denomination

The 1978 Lincoln Cent has a "double denomination" error. Look for a penny design struck over an existing dime, showing elements of both coins. An MS64 example of this rare error sold for **$1,035**.

1979-D Penny Struck on a Dime Planchet

The 1979-D Lincoln Cent has a "wrong planchet" error. Look for a penny design struck on a smaller, silver-colored dime planchet (17.91mm instead of 19.05mm, weighing 2.3g instead of 3.11g). An MS64 example sold for **$1,260**.

1980 Penny Doubled Die Obverse

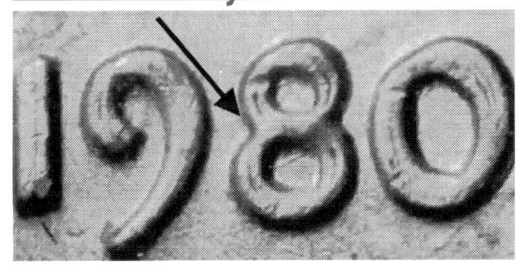

The 1980 Lincoln Cent has a Double Die Obverse (DDO) error. Using magnification, look for clear doubling in the lettering and date on the front of the coin. An MS65 example sold for **$715**.

1982 Penny Value Double Die Error

The 1982 Lincoln Cent has Double Die errors, appearing on both Philadelphia (no mint mark) and Denver pieces. Using magnification, look for doubling in the lettering on both sides, and particularly on Lincoln's ear on Denver coins. Values range from **$150** to **$200** depending on condition.

1983 Penny, Doubled Die Reverse

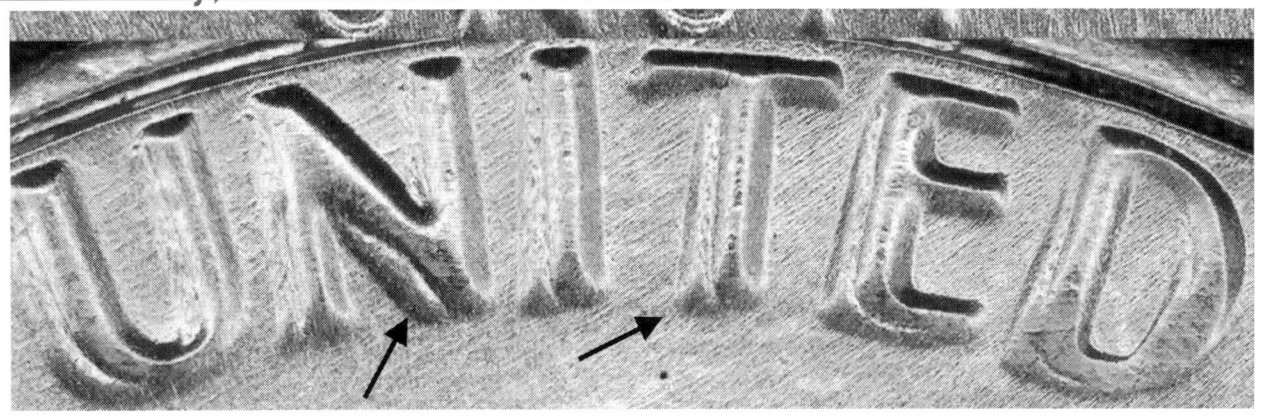

The 1983 Lincoln Cent has a Double Die Reverse (DDR) error. Using magnification, look for doubling in the lettering on the back of the coin - the more prominent the doubling, the higher the value. A pristine red MS68 DDR example reached **$7,050**.

1984 Doubled Die Obverse Penny Error

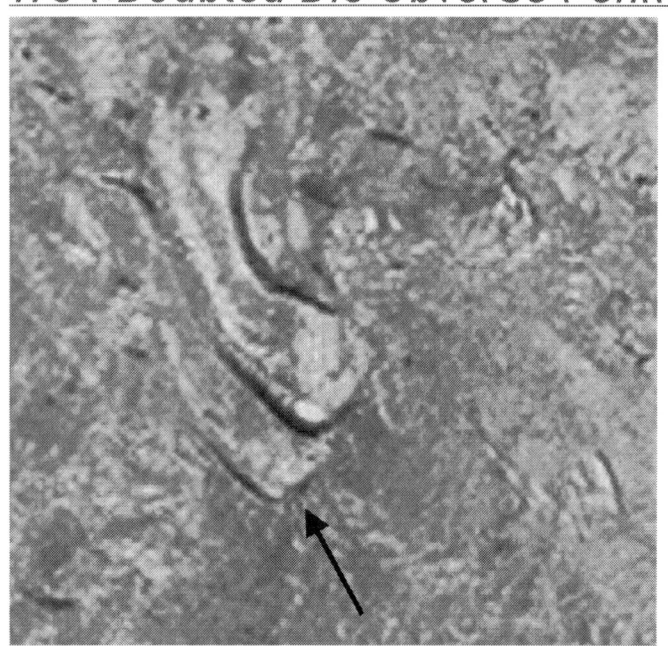

The 1984 Lincoln Cent has a prominent Double Die Obverse error. Even without magnification, look for clear doubling in Lincoln's lower ear, bowtie, and beard. With several thousand examples known, these sell for hundreds of dollars, with the finest example reaching **$3,900**.

1985 No Mint Mark Penny, Partial Plating

The 1985 Lincoln Cent has a "partial plating" error. Look for areas where the grey zinc core is visible through missing copper cladding - particularly over Lincoln's head and lapel, with a diagonal line through the Memorial on the reverse. An MS64 Red-Brown example sold for **$550.**

1986 Wide AM Penny Error

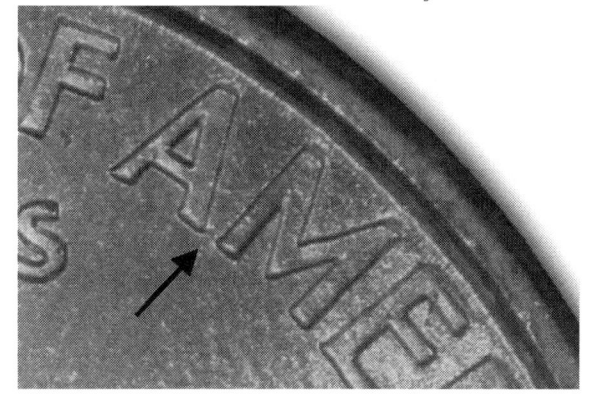

The 1986 Lincoln Cent has a "Wide AM" error. Look at the reverse and check the spacing between the 'A' and 'M' in "AMERICA" - some coins show unusually wide spacing between these letters. In mint state, these errors can sell for up to **$260**.

1988 Penny, Doubled Die Obverse

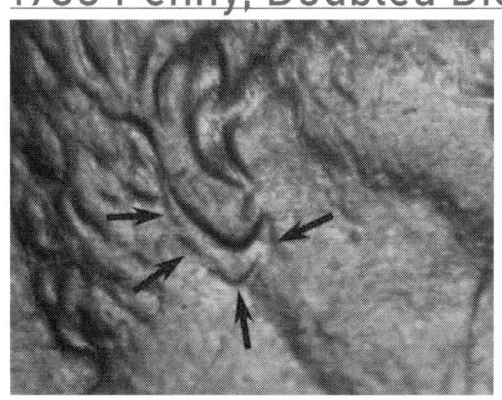

The 1988 Lincoln Cent has Double Die Obverse errors in two varieties: Denver coins show doubling in the "9" of the date, while Philadelphia coins show the valuable "Doubled Ear" variety. A red MS66 example of the Doubled Ear error sold for **$3,120.**

35

1989 – D Penny Struck on a Copper Planchet

The 1989-D Lincoln Cent has a "wrong planchet" error. To identify this rare error, weigh your coin - if it's 3.1 grams (instead of the normal zinc weight), you have one struck on a copper planchet. These rare errors sell for **$3,500** to **$7,500**.

1992 Wide and Close AM Penny Errors

The 1992 Lincoln Cent (both Philadelphia and Denver) has "Wide AM" and "Close AM" errors. On the reverse, look at the spacing between 'A' and 'M' in "AMERICA," and check Gasparro's initials for spacing variations. The "Close AM" variety is rarer - a Philadelphia example sold for **$5,000**, while a Denver piece in AU58 brought **$3,525**.

1993 D Penny, Roosevelt Dime Reverse

The 1993-D Lincoln Cent has an extremely rare "wrong reverse" error. Look for a penny with a normal front but the Roosevelt dime design (torch with olive and oak branches) on the back instead of the Lincoln Memorial. An MS65 Red example of this dramatic error sold for over **$51,000**.

1994 NO Mint Mark Penny DDR

The 1994 Philadelphia Lincoln Cent has a Double Die Reverse error. Using magnification, look for clear doubling in the columns of the Lincoln Memorial on the back. Values range from **$2,050** for an MS67 Red, with a previous MS66 Red example selling for **$2,875**.

1995 No Mint Mark Penny, Double Die Obverse

The 1995 Philadelphia Lincoln Cent has a historic Double Die Obverse error - the last of its kind due to new minting techniques. Look for doubling in the design on the front of the coin. Values range from a few dollars in lower grades to **$4,750** for pristine red MS69 examples.

1998 Penny, Wide AM

The 1998 Lincoln Cent has a "Wide AM" error. On the reverse, look for unusual wide spacing between 'A' and 'M' in "AMERICA" (regular coins have close spacing). Values range from **$10** for circulated pieces to **$940** for pristine red specimens.

1999 Wide AM Penny Error

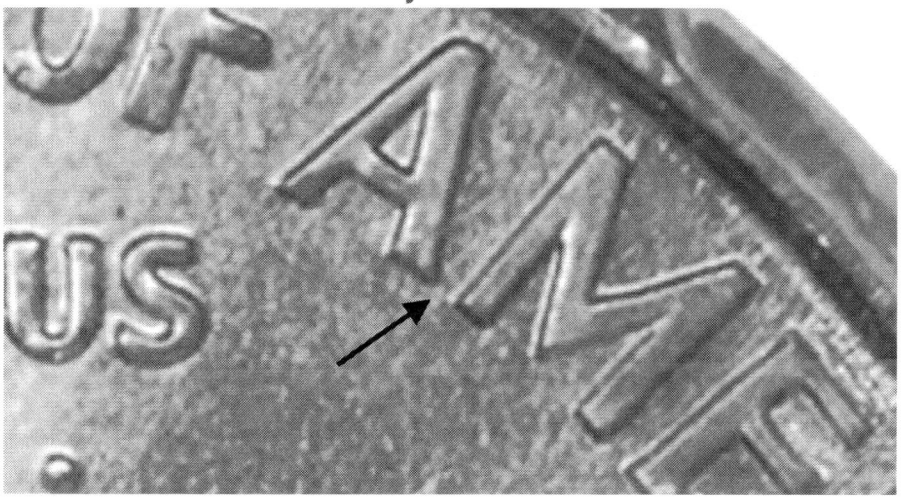

The 1999 Lincoln Cent from Philadelphia and San Francisco has a "Wide AM" error. On the reverse, check the spacing between 'A' and 'M' in "AMERICA" - look for unusually wide spacing created by the accidental use of proof dies. These errors can sell for up to **$300**.

Valuable Jefferson Nickel Errors

Among America's circulation coins, the Jefferson Nickel has proven to be a treasure trove for error collectors. Since its introduction in 1938, replacing the beloved Buffalo design, this five-cent piece has produced some of the most fascinating and valuable mint mistakes in U.S. coinage. While most Jefferson Nickels in your pocket might be worth exactly five cents, certain errors from various years can command prices that would astonish even seasoned collectors.

From dramatic doubled dies to wrong planchets, from striking errors to misaligned dies, these mistakes have become the focus of intense interest among numismatists. Some of these errors occurred during wartime composition changes, while others emerged from the everyday challenges of mass coin production. Whether you're searching through rolls from the bank or inheriting an old collection, knowing what to look for in Jefferson Nickel errors could transform a common coin into a significant find.

1939 (P) Nickel Doubled Monticello DDR

The 1939 Jefferson Nickel has a Double Die Reverse error. Using magnification, look for doubling in "Monticello" and "Five Cents" on the back of the coin. Values range from **$4,600** to **$23,500** for top-grade specimens (MS67 and above).

1940 S Repunched Mint Mark Nickel Error

The 1940-S Jefferson Nickel has a repunched mint mark error. Using magnification, look for a doubled or tripled "S" mint mark showing overlapping impressions. Values range from **$45** in XF45 condition to **$800** for MS68 specimens.

1941 Jefferson Nickel, Re-punched Mint Mark

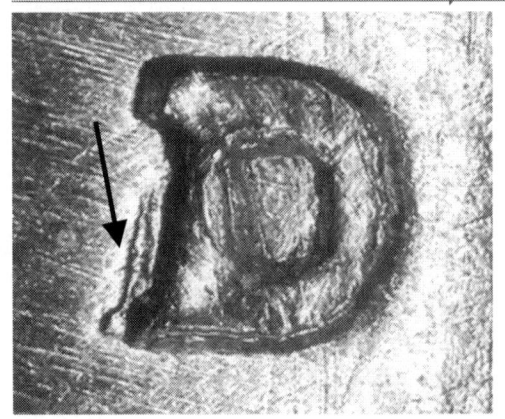

The 1941 Jefferson Nickel has repunched mint mark errors. Using magnification, look for mint marks showing multiple impressions in different positions (upside-down, sideways, or faint). Common varieties sell for **$3-$5**, while dramatic errors can reach **$20-$25**.

1941 Jefferson Nickel, Off-center

The 1941 Jefferson Nickel has "off-center" strike errors. Look for coins with part of the design missing along one edge - 5-10% off-center brings **$8-$15**, while 50% off-center with visible date can fetch **$75-$100**.

1942 Jefferson Nickel, Re-punched Mint Mark

The 1942 Jefferson Nickel has repunched mint mark errors, with the "D over horizontal D" being most valuable. Using magnification, look for a D mint mark struck twice at a 90-degree angle. Values range from **$135** to **$32,200**, with Full Steps specimens bringing the highest prices. The Philadelphia (P/P) variety in MS66 has sold for **$1,050**.

41

1943 Jefferson Nickel, Double Die Obverse (doubled-eye)

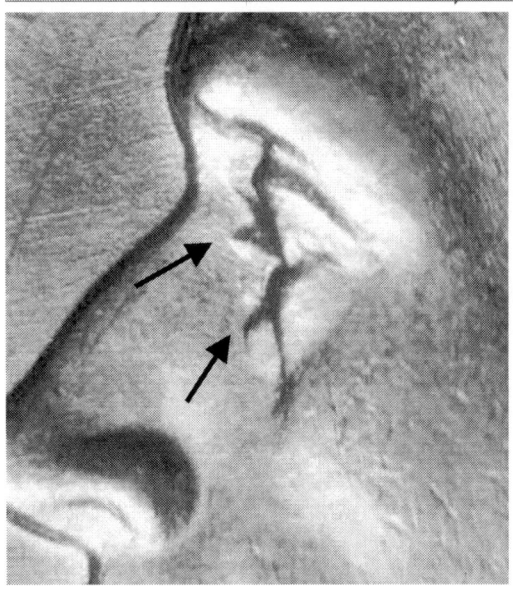

The 1943-P Jefferson Nickel has a "Doubled Eye" error. Look for doubling in Jefferson's left eye - some examples are visible to the naked eye, while others require magnification. Values range from **$35** to **$11,500**, with Full Steps specimens commanding the highest prices.

1944 Jefferson Nickel, Re-punched Mint Mark

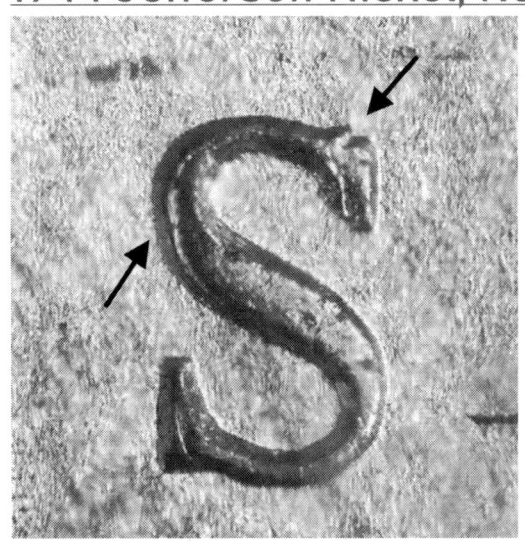

The 1944 Jefferson Nickel has repunched mint mark errors (both D and S mints). Using magnification, look for mint marks showing multiple strikes in different positions. Common examples sell for a few dollars, while premium specimens with Full Steps can reach **$750**.

42

1948 S Jefferson Nickel, Off-center

The 1968 Jefferson Nickel has "off-center" strike errors. Look for coins with part of the design missing and a blank crescent-shaped area. Values vary by severity: 5-10% off-center brings **$3-$10**, while 50% off-center with visible date can fetch over **$75.**

1952-D Nickel Broadstruck Cleaned

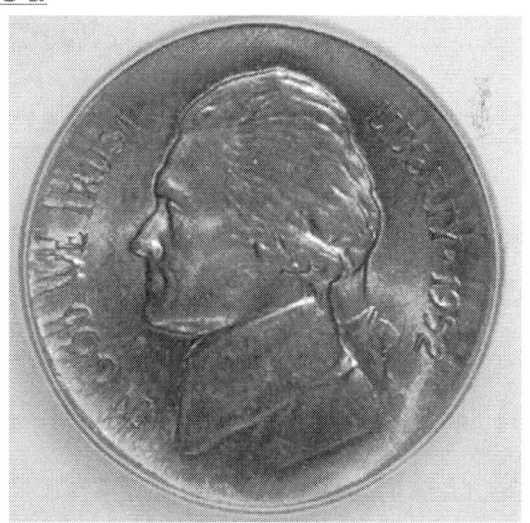

The 1952-D Jefferson Nickel has a "broadstruck" error. Look for coins without a defined rim, appearing wider and flatter than normal. A cleaned MS60 example sold for **$70**, though uncleaned specimens would be worth more.

1952 (P) Nickel Broken Planchet – 2 Pieces

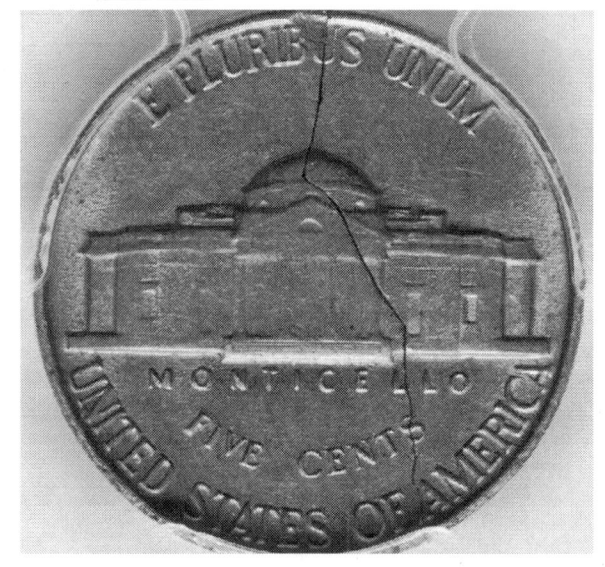

The 1952 Philadelphia Jefferson Nickel has a "split planchet" error. Look for coins that split into two matching pieces like a puzzle. A paired set in AU58 condition sold for **$180**.

1952 (P) Nickel Struck on a Dime Planchet

The 1952 Philadelphia Jefferson Nickel has a "wrong planchet" error. Look for a nickel design struck on a smaller dime planchet (17.91mm instead of 21.21mm, weighing 2.4g instead of 5g) with cut-off design elements. An AU55 example sold for **$470**.

1952 (P) Nickel Struck on a Penny Planchet

The 1952 Philadelphia Jefferson Nickel has a "wrong planchet" error. Look for a nickel design struck on a smaller, copper-colored penny planchet (19.05mm instead of 21.21mm) with cut-off design elements. An MS63 Brown example sold for **$600**.

1955 Nickel D over S

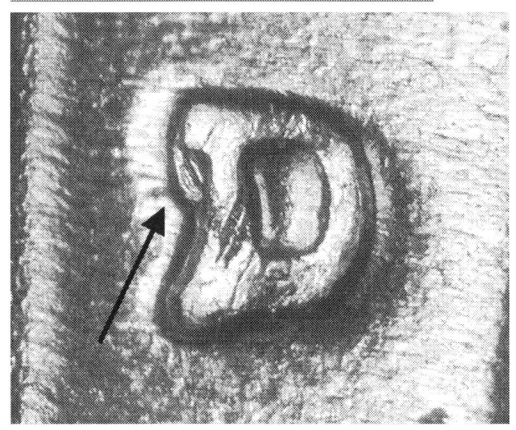

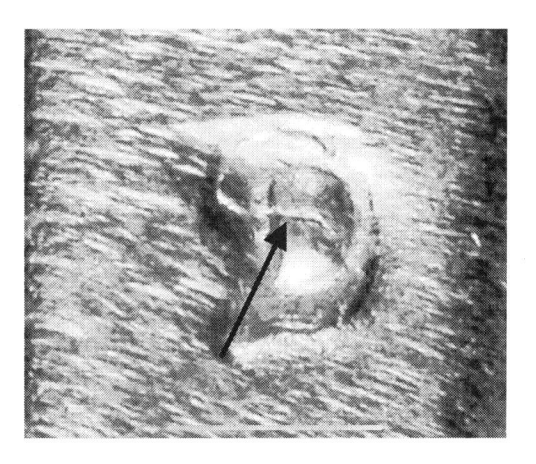

The 1955-D Jefferson Nickel has an intentional "D over S" mint mark variety. Using magnification, look for the top of an "S" visible above the "D" mint mark. Values range from **$5** for circulated pieces to **$3,738** for pristine MS66 examples.

1959 Nickel Struck on a Silver Dime Planchet

The 1959 Jefferson Nickel has a "wrong planchet" error. Look for a nickel design struck on a smaller silver dime planchet (17.91mm instead of 21.21mm) with cut-off design elements. These rare errors typically sell for over **$600**.

1960 No Mint Mark Nickel Struck on a 1-Cent Planchet

The 1960 Philadelphia Jefferson Nickel has a "wrong planchet" error. Look for a nickel design struck on a copper-colored penny planchet with cut-off design elements. An MS64 Red-Brown example sold for nearly **$500**.

1963-D Nickel Struck on a Dime Planchet

The 1963-D Jefferson Nickel has a "wrong planchet" error. Look for a nickel design struck on a smaller silver dime planchet (weighing 2.6g instead of 5g) with cut-off design elements. An MS62 example sold for **$550**.

1964 Nickel Struck On a 10-Centavo Coin Error

The 1964 Jefferson Nickel has a rare "wrong planchet" error. Look for a nickel design struck on a Philippine 10-centavo planchet, weighing half of a normal nickel. An MS64 example sold for **$1,200**.

1966 Nickel Struck on 10C Planchet Error

The 1966 Jefferson Nickel has "wrong planchet" errors struck on either dime or penny planchets. Look for nickel designs on smaller planchets showing cut-off design elements. Dime planchet errors in AU58 sold for over **$300**, while penny planchet errors in MS64 Red-Brown reached over **$800**.

1970 S Nickel, Double Struck and Broadstruck

The 1970-S Jefferson Nickel has a combination of "double strike," "broadstrike," and "struck-through" errors. Look for a coin with spread metal beyond its normal edge, multiple strike impressions, and partially obscured design from being struck through another planchet. An MS67 Full Steps example paired with its companion die cap error sold for over **$2,000**.

Valuable Roosevelt Dime Errors

In the realm of modern U.S. coinage, the Roosevelt Dime stands out as a fascinating hunting ground for error collectors. Since its introduction in 1946, honoring the recently departed President Franklin D. Roosevelt, this ten-cent piece has produced some of the most intriguing and valuable mint mistakes. While most dimes in circulation are worth exactly ten cents, certain errors have sold for thousands of dollars, turning pocket change into numismatic treasures.

From dramatic die clashes to wrong planchets, from striking errors to composition mistakes, these tiny coins have developed an impressive catalog of valuable variations. Whether examining silver dimes from the early years or more recent clad issues, knowing what to look for could mean the difference between spending a dime and discovering a four-figure rarity. Let's explore these fascinating mistakes that have become the pride of error coin collections.

1951 Dime Re-punched Mint Mark Error

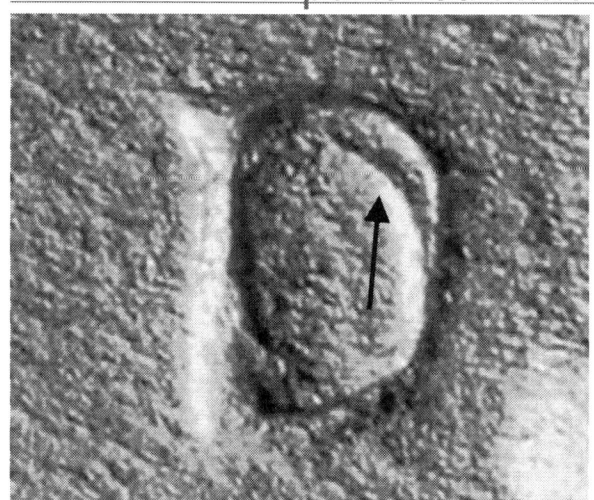

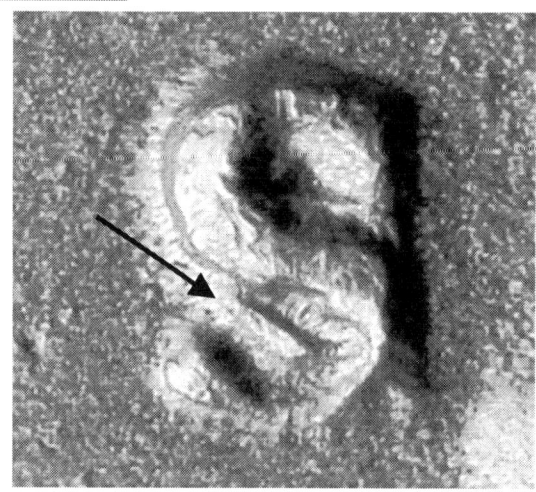

The 1961 Roosevelt Dime has a repunched mint mark error. Using magnification, look for doubled "D" or "S" mint marks. An MS65 Full Bands example sold for **$70**.

1968 Dime, Doubled Die

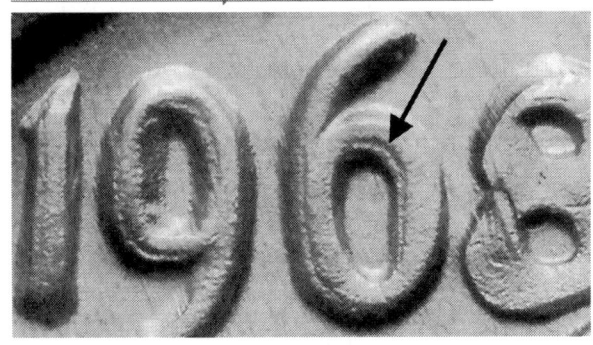

The 1968 Roosevelt Dime has a Double Die error. Using magnification, look for clear doubling in the design. Values range from **$65** to **$160** depending on condition.

1964 Doubled Die Obverse Dime Error

The 1964 Roosevelt Dime has a Double Die error. Using magnification, look for doubling in "IN GOD WE TRUST" and the date. A Proof 68 example sold for **$1,100**.

1946 Dime, Re-punched Mint Mark (D/D or S/S)

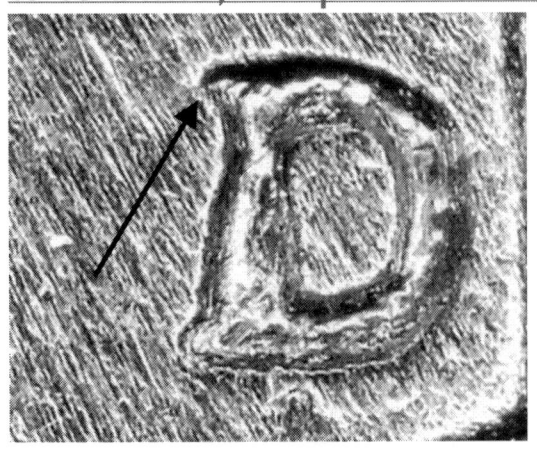

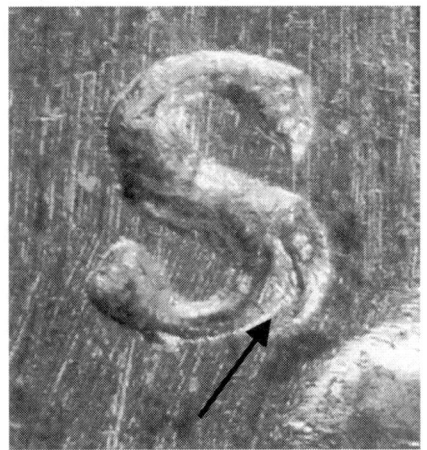

The 1946 Roosevelt Dime has repunched mint mark errors from both Denver and San Francisco mints. Using magnification, look for doubled or tripled "D" or "S" mint marks. Values range from $50-$150 for common varieties, with Full Bands specimens selling for **$380-$995**, and San Francisco varieties reaching several thousand dollars.

1946 Dime, Doubled-die Obverse/Reverse

The 1946 Philadelphia Roosevelt Dime has Double Die errors on both obverse (DDO) and reverse (DDR). Using magnification, look for doubling in numbers and lettering. Values range from $135 for basic specimens to $2,760 for Full Bands pieces with combined DDR and repunched mint mark errors.

1946 Dime Struck on an Elliptical Planchet

The 1946 Roosevelt Dime has an "elliptical planchet" error. Look for dimes with an oval shape instead of the normal circular shape. One example sold for **$260.**

1965 Dime Broad strike

The 1965 Roosevelt Dime has a "broadstrike" error. Look for coins without a defined rim but with complete designs on both sides. An MS65 example sold for approximately **$80**.

Valuable Washington Quarter Errors

Among U.S. coins, the Washington Quarter has proven to be particularly fertile ground for error collectors. Since its debut in 1932, replacing the Standing Liberty design, this twenty-five cent piece has produced some of the most valuable and fascinating mint errors in American numismatics. While most quarters in your pocket might be worth exactly twenty-five cents, certain minting mistakes have transformed ordinary quarters into five-figure rarities.

The series spans multiple design changes, from the original eagle reverse to the State Quarters Program and beyond, creating unique opportunities for errors across different eras. Whether it's dramatic double dies, off-center strikes, wrong planchets, or the infamous "In God We Rust" variety, these mistakes have become highly sought after by collectors. Some of the most remarkable finds have come from everyday people who simply knew what to look for.

Let's explore these valuable errors that could be hiding in your change or collection. After all, the difference between spending a quarter and finding a valuable error could simply be knowing what to look for.

1966 Quarter, Magnetic Wire Struck in Obverse

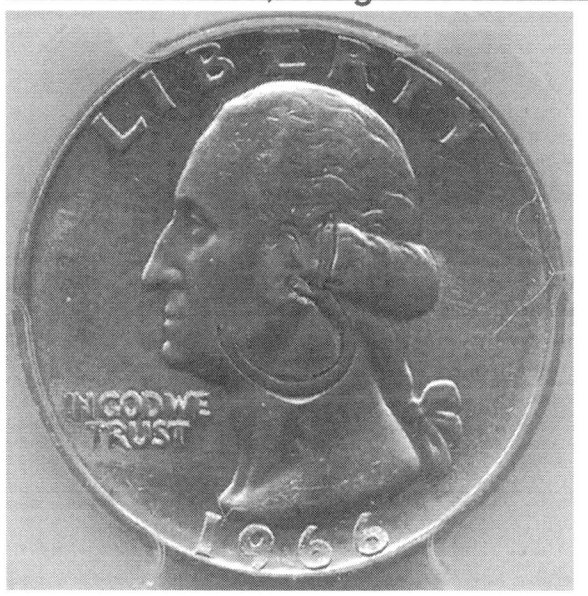

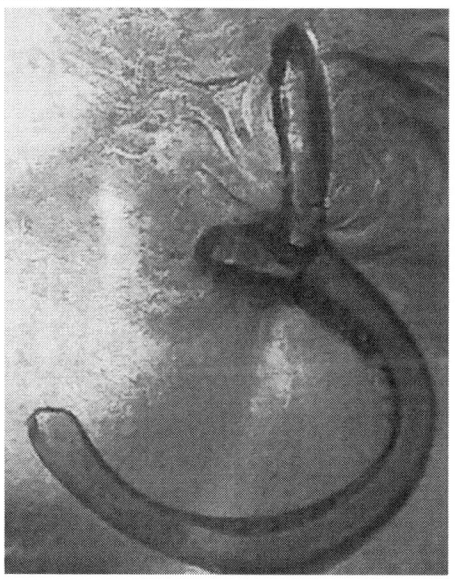

The 1968 Washington Quarter has a "wire struck-through" error. Look for a horseshoe-shaped impression from a wire embedded in the coin's front design. One example sold for over **$600**.

1966 Quarter, DDR

The 1972 Washington Quarter has a Double Die Reverse error. Using magnification, look for clear doubling in the design elements on the back of the coin - more obvious doubling means higher value. An XF45 example sold for **$920**.

1966 Quarter Struck on a Dime Planchet

The 1975 Washington Quarter has a "wrong planchet" error. Look for a quarter design struck on a smaller dime planchet, showing cut-off design elements. These errors can sell for up to **$300**.

1943 Silver Quarter Double Die Error

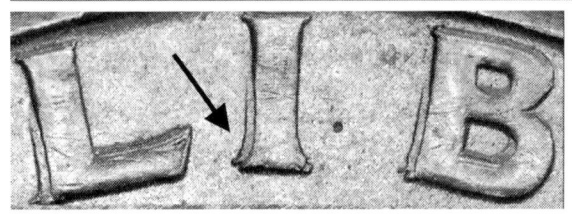

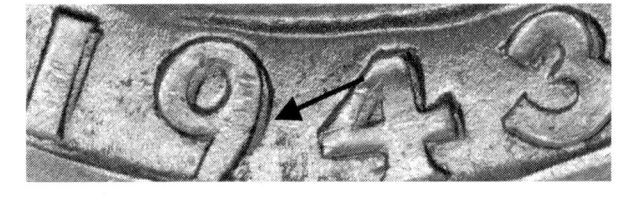

The 1943 Washington Quarter has Double Die Obverse errors from both Philadelphia and San Francisco mints. Using magnification, look for overlapping in design elements on the front. Values range from **$200-$2,750** for circulated pieces up to **$12,000** for pristine MS65 Philadelphia specimens.

1963 Quarter, Double Die Obverse

The 1963 Washington Quarter (both Philadelphia and Denver) has Double Die Obverse errors. Using magnification, look for shifted or doubled design elements on the front. Values range from **$552** for an MS65 Denver piece to **$1,680** for a pristine MS67+ Philadelphia example.

1963 Quarter, Double Die Reverse

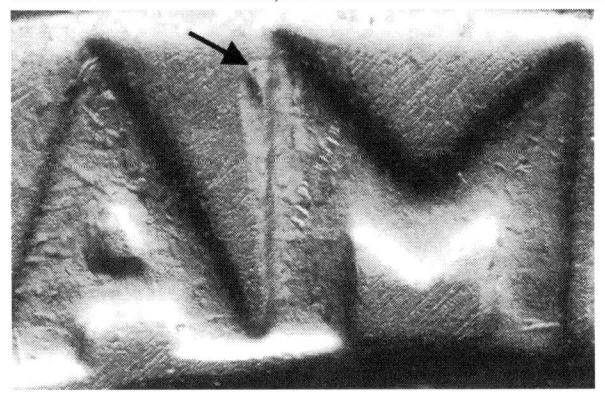

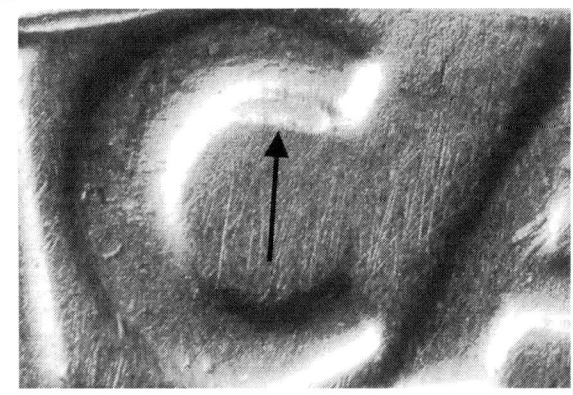

The 1963 Washington Quarter has a Double Die Reverse error. Using magnification, look for doubled letters or design elements on the back of the coin. An MS65 example sold for **$720**.

1963 D Quarter Struck on a Cent Planchet

The 1963-D Washington Quarter has a "wrong planchet" error. Look for a quarter design struck on a smaller, copper-colored penny planchet (weighing 3.03g instead of normal weight) with cut-off design elements. An MS65 Brown example sold for **$1,300**.

1950 D Quarter Re-punched Mint Mark Error

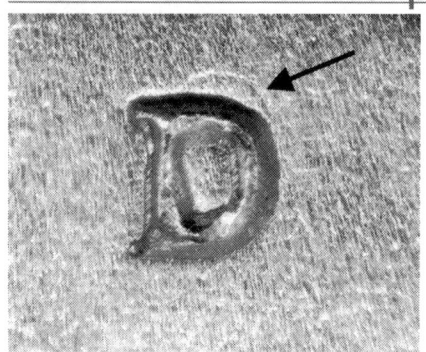

The 1950-D Washington Quarter has a repunched mint mark error. Using magnification, look for a doubled "D" mint mark struck at different angles. Values range from **$40** in AU55 condition to **$150** in MS65.

1950 Quarter D over S Mint Mark Error

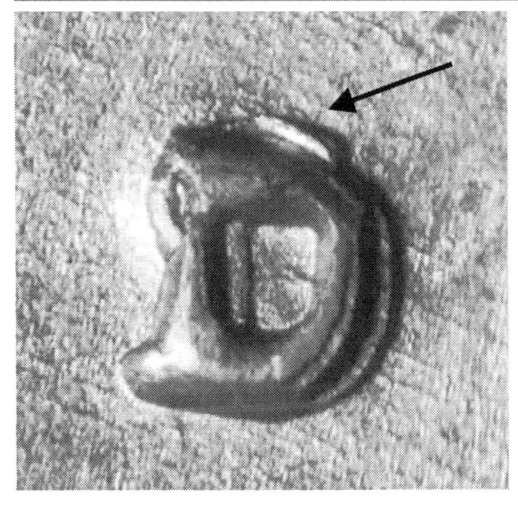

The 1950 Washington Quarter has a "D over S" mint mark error. Using magnification, look for traces of an "S" mint mark visible beneath the "D." Values range from **$150** in AU55 condition to **$3,500** in MS65.

1950 Quarter Double Die Reverse Error

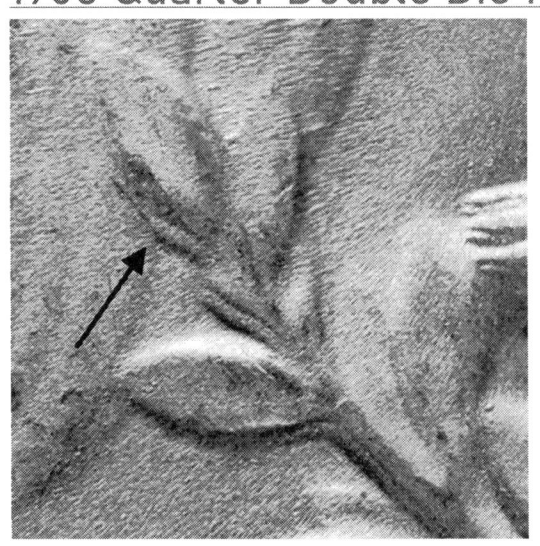

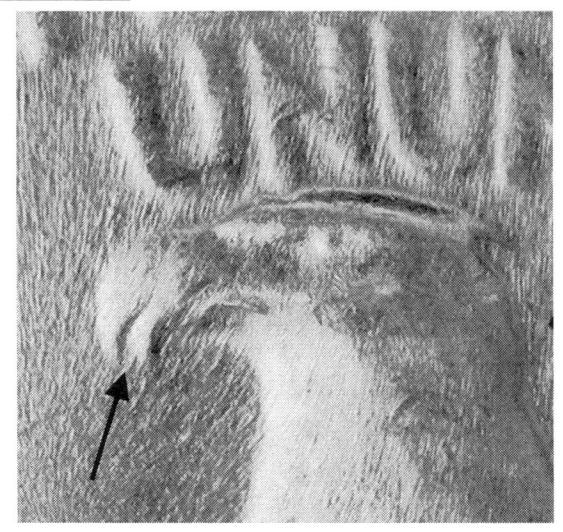

The 1950 Washington Quarter (both Philadelphia and Denver) has Double Die Reverse errors. Using magnification, look for doubled design elements on the back of the coin. Values range from **$25** in AU55 condition to **$150** for an MS65 Denver specimen.

1964 Quarter, Doubled Die Reverse Error

The 1964 Washington Quarter has multiple Double Die Reverse varieties (FS-801 through 804) from both Philadelphia and Denver mints. Using magnification, look for doubled design elements on the back. Values range from **$385** for Denver MS65 specimens to **$1,920** for the rarest Philadelphia FS-801 variety.

1964 Quarter, Doubled Die Obverse Error

The 1964 Washington Quarter has Double Die Obverse errors from both Philadelphia and Denver mints. Using magnification, look for doubled design elements on the front of the coin. Values range from **$228** for Philadelphia MS65 specimens to **$500** for Denver MS65 examples.

1932 Quarter, Doubled Die Obverse

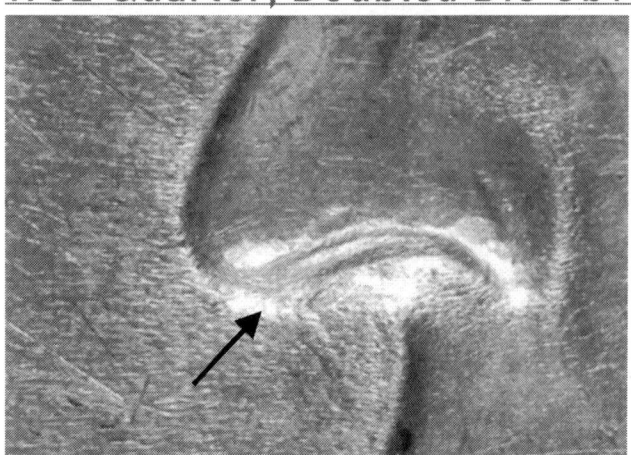

The 1982 Washington Quarter has a Double Die Obverse error. Using magnification, look for doubled design elements on the front of the coin. Values range from **$250** to **$1,000**, with the finest known MS66 example selling for **$3,055**.

Valuable Kennedy Half-Dollar Errors

Among America's modern coinage, the Kennedy Half Dollar stands as a unique canvas for mint errors. Since its rushed introduction in 1964, mere months after President Kennedy's assassination, this fifty-cent piece has produced some of the most valuable and fascinating mistakes in U.S. numismatics. While most Kennedy halves in circulation might be worth their face value, certain minting errors have transformed these memorial coins into five-figure treasures.

From dramatic doubled dies to composition errors, from striking mistakes to wrong planchets, these large coins have developed an impressive catalog of valuable variations. The series spans multiple metallic compositions - from 90% silver to 40% silver to copper-nickel clad - creating unique opportunities for errors across different eras. Some of the most remarkable finds have come from everyday collectors who simply knew what distinctive features to look for.

Let's explore these valuable errors that could be hiding in your collection. After all, the difference between spending fifty cents and discovering a significant numismatic treasure often comes down to knowing exactly what makes these errors special.

1964-D/D Re-punched Mint Mark

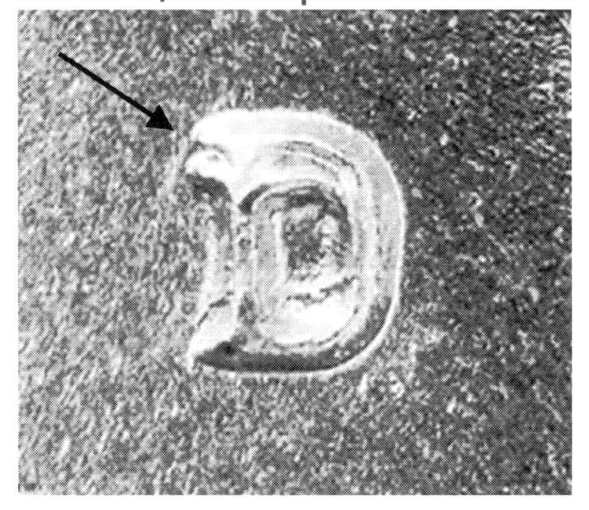

The 1963-D Kennedy Half Dollar has a repunched mint mark error. Using magnification, look for a doubled "D" mint mark showing overlapping impressions. An MS66 example sold for **$400**.

1964-D Double Die Obverse

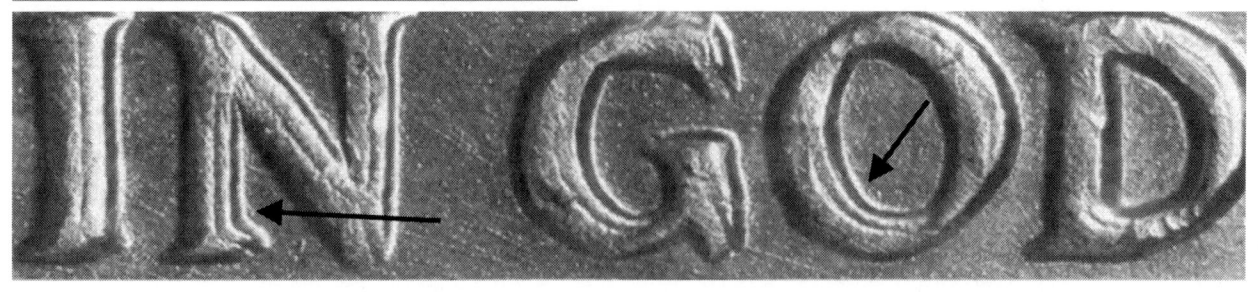

The 1964-D Kennedy Half Dollar has a Double Die Obverse error. Using magnification, look for doubled design elements on the front of the coin. Values start at **$225** for mint state examples.

1972 D "No FG" Half Dollar

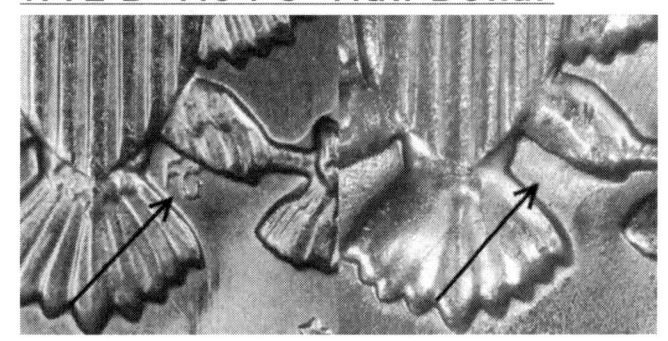

The 1972-D Kennedy Half Dollar has a "Missing FG" error. On the reverse, look for the complete absence of the designer's initials "FG" between the eagle's tail feathers and right leg. Values range from **$60** in low grades up to **$4,500** for the finest MS66 specimen.

1972 No Mint Mark Half Dollar, Double Die Obverse

The 1972 Philadelphia Kennedy Half Dollar has Double Die Obverse errors. Using magnification, look for doubling in "IN GOD WE TRUST." Values range from **$40** in XF45 condition to **$850** for MS65 specimens.

1971 Half Dollar Double Die Error

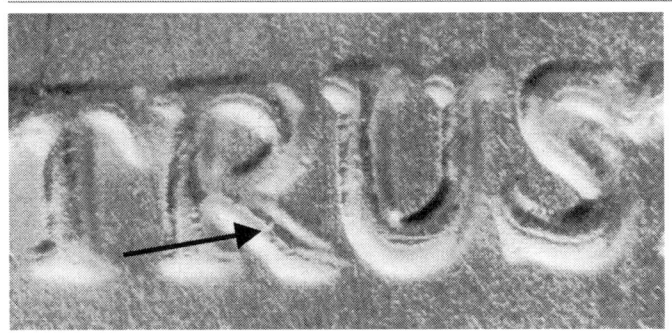

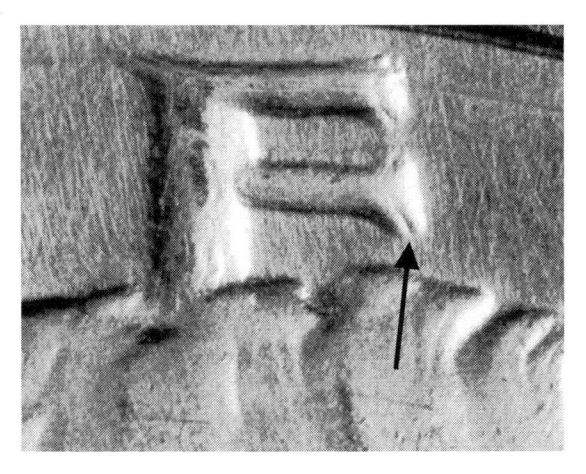

The 1971 Kennedy Half Dollar has Double Die errors on both obverse and reverse. Using magnification, look for doubled letters, numbers, and mint marks on either side. These errors can sell for **$2,000** or more.

1977-D Half Dollar DDO Error

The 1975 Kennedy Half Dollar has a Double Die Obverse error. Using magnification, look for doubled design elements on the front of the coin. An MS65 example sold for **$800**, with current value around **$750**.

1977-D Half Dollar Struck on a 40% Silver Planchet

The 1977-D Kennedy Half Dollar has a "wrong planchet" error. Look for a half dollar struck on a 40% silver planchet (meant for 1976 Bicentennial coins) instead of the normal copper-nickel composition. An AU58 example sold for **$6,600**.

CHAPTER 6

MARKET NAVIGATION

Price Guides and Resources

In the ever-evolving world of error coin collecting, having access to accurate and up-to-date pricing information is crucial for making informed decisions. Whether you're buying, selling, or simply evaluating your finds, knowing current market values can mean the difference between a good deal and a missed opportunity.

Scan this code to access our comprehensive digital resource package:

- U.S Coin Identification Guide
- Error Coins Identification Guide
- Price Guide to Mint Errors

These digital resources will help you stay current with market trends and make informed collecting decisions.

Where To Sell Your Coins

Finding the right place to sell your error coins takes time, but selecting the appropriate marketplace will maximize your chances of a successful sale. Let's explore your main options:

Facebook
http://www.facebook.com

Facebook hosts numerous coin trading groups where collectors buy, sell, and trade coins. Popular groups include CoinBook, Coin Pro, and Error and Varieties communities. Be sure to check each group's specific guidelines before participating.

eBAY - Collectibles -Coins
www.ebay.com

USA Coin Book
http://www.usacoinbook.com/

At USA Coin Book, there are absolutely no listing fees and a very low 2% final value fee. That means it is totally free to list all of your coins up for sale or put them on auctions for as long as you like.

Coin World Marketplace
https://www.coinworld.com

NGC Collectors Society
coins.www.collectors-society.com

CONECA Members Share
board.conecaonline.org

Numismatics News
https://www.numismaticnews.net

CHAPTER 7

Strategies for Selling Your Error Coins

If you've made it this far into exploring error coins, you've likely started examining your pocket change with newfound interest. Over time, you'll accumulate coins that you've properly identified and are ready to "cash in," or perhaps you've been bitten by the collecting bug and want to acquire more varieties. Either way, understanding how to navigate the buying and selling process is crucial.

Error-variety coin collecting remains an obscure specialty to most dealers. Many will offer minimal amounts or show no interest at all. However, don't be discouraged – thousands of collectors eagerly seek these pieces, and a network of specialized dealers exists to serve this market. The key is knowing how to connect with them.

Your first decision is choosing how to sell your coins. Three main avenues exist: selling to dealers, direct to collectors, or through auctions. Each path has distinct advantages and challenges.

Selling to dealers offers immediate closure – you're done once you cash their check. The dealer handles everything else: finding buyers, packaging, shipping, pricing research, grading, and marketing. They'll also serve as a qualified examiner, verifying your attributions. However, be prepared for lower offers since dealers need room for profit.

Before diving in, you must understand proper attribution. Many forms of doubling mimic collectible varieties but are virtually worthless. For instance, acid-soaked coins might appear to be wrong planchet strikes, and "magician's coins" (two pieces lathed together) hold only novelty value. Misidentifying these can damage your reputation irreparably.

When approaching dealers, phone calls work best for gauging interest quickly. Some specialize in major striking errors like off-centers and clips, while others focus on die varieties. If writing, always include a self-addressed stamped envelope and detailed descriptions referencing standard attribution guides. This courtesy, combined with demonstrated knowledge, significantly improves your chances of a favorable response.

Once comfortable working with dealers and confident in your attributions, consider selling directly to collectors. Create detailed listings clearly describing each piece, including attribution numbers and grades. Offer reasonable return policies – 7 to 14 days is standard, but three days is too short. Keep shipping charges fair; $2-3 is reasonable, $7 isn't.

Auctions provide another avenue, particularly for significant pieces. While major auction houses typically handle only high-value items, specialized error coin clubs offer auction services at modest costs. These venues provide the added benefit of expert examination before listing, though they won't do detailed attributions.

Online auctions have revolutionized coin selling. Sites like eBay offer tremendous reach, but success requires accurate descriptions, quality images, and established credibility. Study successful sellers' listings and presentation methods before venturing into this arena.

Remember, reputation is everything in numismatics. Never knowingly sell misattributed pieces, maintain fair policies, and continuously educate yourself. Building trust with dealers and collectors creates long-term opportunities in this fascinating specialty.

The most critical rule: deal only in properly attributed coins. Building a solid reputation through honest dealings will serve you far better than quick profits from questionable pieces. Take time to learn the market, understand the material, and establish relationships with reputable dealers and collectors. Success follows naturally from this foundation.

BONUS CHAPTER

Congratulations! As a reader of this guide, you've unlocked access to a carefully curated collection of exclusive resources that will elevate your error coin collecting journey. What you're about to discover goes beyond the pages of this book – it's your gateway to insider knowledge and expert communities.

I've assembled an exclusive package that includes:

Private Coin Collector Communities

Gain direct access to specialized groups where experienced collectors share their discoveries, knowledge, and insights. These aren't just regular forums – they're carefully vetted communities where real expertise flows freely.

Exclusive Video Masterclass: The Complete Collector's Guide

Step into our premium video vault where seasoned numismatists share their closely guarded secrets. This comprehensive video series transforms complex collecting concepts into clear, actionable knowledge.

FREE Digital Edition: Valuable United States Coins 2025

Your exclusive digital copy of the most up-to-date coin valuation guide, ensuring you always know current market values. **SCAN THE CODE BELOW TO GAIN ACCESS!**

I Value Your Feedback!

Thank you for choosing this guide to enhance your coin collecting journey. Your satisfaction is my top priority, and I'd love to hear about your experience with this book.

Please take a moment to leave your feedback on Amazon. Your honest opinion is incredibly important to me and the coin collecting community. Thank you for your support and happy collecting!

FOR MORE OF MY BOOKS ON COIN & ERROR COLLECTING, SCAN CODE BELOW:

APPENDICES

Glossary of Terms and Definitions

In the specialized world of numismatics, mastering key terminology is essential for effective communication with dealers and fellow collectors. Here's your comprehensive guide to essential coin terminology:

D, S, P Mint Marks - These letters indicate where a coin was produced: Denver (D), San Francisco (S), or Philadelphia (P). The D mark has historical significance, also used for gold coins from Dahlonega (1838-1861).

Alloy - The scientific blending of multiple metals in their molten state. For instance, bronze combines copper, tin, and zinc.

ANA (American Numismatic Association) - The world's leading organization dedicated to coin education, welcoming dealers, collectors, and researchers alike.

BIE Error - A distinctive die break occurring between B and E in LIBERTY on Lincoln cents, creating what appears as an "I".

Blank/Planchet - A metal disc prepared for striking. Once its edge is raised, it's called a planchet.

BREEN Numbers - Attribution numbers established by Walter Breen in his "Complete Encyclopedia of U.S. & Colonial Coins" (1996).

Business Strike - Regular coins intended for everyday circulation.

Central Design - The primary image on either side of a coin. For example, Kennedy's portrait dominates the half dollar's obverse.

Cherrypick - The art of discovering rare varieties being offered as common coins.

Clad Coinage - Modern coins constructed with layers of different metals. Current dimes through half dollars feature a copper core between copper-nickel layers.

CONECA - Combined Organization of Numismatic Error Collectors of America, the authority on error and variety coins.

Die Clash - Occurs when dies strike each other without a planchet between them, transferring designs between faces.

Die Crack - A raised, irregular line on the coin resulting from a crack in the die.

Die Break (Cud) - A major die failure creating a raised blob, often likened to a tobacco chewer's "cud".

Die Life - The productive lifespan of a die, measured by coins struck before retirement.

Die Stage - Documents progressive die deterioration through chips, cracks, and clashes.

Die State - Rates die condition from "very early" (VEDS) to "very late" (VLDS).

Die Trails - Doubling effect creating "wavy steps" on Lincoln cents due to single squeeze minting.

Die Variety - Collectible variations in coin design from production changes or mishaps.

Double Denomination - When a coin receives strikes from dies of two different denominations.

DDO (Doubled Die Obverse) - Doubling on the front from hub misalignment.

DDR (Doubled Die Reverse) - Similar doubling but on the coin's reverse.

Off Metal Error - Wrong planchet composition, like a cent struck on dime planchet.

Multiple Variety - A coin showing more than one distinct error type.

Grade - Overall coin condition, considering wear, luster, marks, strike quality, and eye appeal

Mint State (MS) - Unworn coin showing no circulation, may have natural toning

Uncirculated - Coin without wear, potentially brilliant or toned

Oxidation - Natural surface tarnish from environmental exposure

Circulated - Shows wear from public use

Proof - Specially struck collector coin with mirror-like fields and frosted designs

Repunched Mintmark (RPM) - Multiple visible impressions of the same mintmark

Planchet - Prepared blank ready for striking

Strike - The process of impressing designs onto the planchet

Working Die - The actual die striking coins

Working Hub - Creates working dies from master die

Legend - All inscriptions except date and denomination

Rim - Raised border between design field and coin edge

Collar - Controls metal flow during striking to form proper edge

Made in United States
Troutdale, OR
01/23/2025